Making Spirit Real

By Tom King

Published by New Generation Publishing in 2021

First Edition

ISBN 978-1-80031-296-8

www.newgeneration-publishing.com

Introduction

The contents of this book are for anyone who feels a little lost and alone. It is my honest account of growing up and realising the energies around me, becoming psychically aware can be quite scary. Your sensitivity levels are lifted off the scale. Compassion and empathy will become your new friends too for awhile you will feel like you're treading on egg shells with every situation. But slowly you will come to realise that on your personal journey these signposts are for your growth and wellness. We must always do what we think is right at the time and the experiences of this will make us better people. I hope you enjoy this book and just accept it for what it is “My Opinion” on a spiritual life and becoming aware that there is more than this. From one single candle we can light thousands - may this be a light to show you - your way .

Chapter one :

The Early Years

I thought I was no different to anyone else. The world I saw was the same for everyone. How wrong I was. My childhood was happy - but to be honest I did not seem to be part of IT….. the world rolled by at 100 miles an hour and I just seemed very distanced from the here and now. My Junior School years were OK but I was very mixed up with things in my head. Why the vivid dreams and why all the sleepwalking and talking. This all came to a head one Christmas 1970 it was the day of my Christmas party all was good with cakes and trifle. I loved the simple things in life - Christmas music was playing and fun and laughter filled the room - I noticed the bright lights seem to bother me and I developed a banging headache - in time I became violently sick. I was taken home obviously as I felt I had picked up a bug. The next few days I was wondering in and out of consciousness I could not quench my thirst .. My dad phoned our doctors but he would not come out - I became very weak and slept most of the time - what sort of a bug was this? Surely tomorrow would be better.

Luckily one of the neighbours had been a Sister in a large hospital in Yorkshire - she came to see me and immediately saw a very grave situation.

I was flown by Ambucopter to Sheffield Children's Hospital barely alive and swaying between the two worlds. Many doctors working frantically my limp body had slipped into a deep coma. The Diagnosis "Meningitis" The worst strain - pumped full of drugs and left in the hands of the almighty - was this my time to take a bow?

Eighteen days later I awoke with tubes everywhere and a feeling of complete and utter nothing. I did not recognise anything - people were talking and asking questions but all I wanted to do was sleep.

My parents visited me although they were in the same room I felt lost and alone. I remember looking in the mirror at this reflection not knowing who or what I was.

The next few days passed quickly but I still felt numb and thrown back into a world I did not know.I seemed sensitive to everything and could not come to terms with all these constant voices.

The hospital saved my life and for that I will be eternally grateful.

Back home my family did a Christmas party with balloons and streamers everywhere. I had missed all of Christmas and New Year. It was lovely to see everyone and to be back home. Something had changed within me I became withdrawn from this physical world and seemed to be alone. My dreams continued but seemed to last forever even when I was awake. a lot to take in - too much - thoughts of things that had happened whilst I was in a coma. But how could this be right I was unconscious .....wasn't I.

I would see many specialists afterwards keeping a check on an 8 year old boy - most said my recovery was remarkable - considering the seriousness of the situation - but the world had changed or had I changed ?

Senior years :

When it was time to move on up to big school as I called it - I felt nervous and anxious. Too many people to contend with as well as the countless voices in my head.

It was a good school but my favorite part was P.E. I loved sport and could express myself there - football was my passion and I was an OK player and made the school team. To be part of a team felt so good and I loved it.

The rest of the lessons meant very little to me and often had days off feeling unwell. My teachers for the main were excellent but I felt detached and not worthy really of any ones attention - school reports spoke well but my interests were dying each term.

Socially I was not a good mixer, preferred being alone - much safer - I was close to several friends but knew these were friendships of convenience - and so I meandered through school mainly alone or so I thought.

Living in the country I would often go on long walks it was comforting just me and nature along the way I would meet the occasional dog walker - we would smile and nod at each other - peace with nature was wonderful. On such a walk I met a girl called Claire I saw her walking her white terrier dog she was happy and smiling and we chatted for a few minutes about everything and nothing, the next day I came downstairs to find the curtains still drawn. It was 10:00 o'clock a lovely sunny day - my Mum explained that a young girl who had been tragically killed in a car accident two weeks ago and today her funeral courtage was passing our house. In respect I went outside and bowed my head - there were flowers all over a coffin one such spelt out her name Claire in beautiful white flowers, how could this be possible? A neighbour knew the girl she had past some sixteen days ago, my mind was fried what was going on? She said that she was devoted to her white terrier dog who had past earlier this year.

I smiled and realised that these two beautiful souls had found themselves again reunited in heaven. So my mind wasn't playing games this was for real, having passed through the veil and then push back into reality the spirit world had other desires and plans for me I didn't choose them ….they chose me ….

Exams came and went I did OK but lacked the concentration to go further. One night having just fallen asleep I was awoken by my Auntie at the side of my bed, I did not seem to find this strange especially as she lived sixty miles away. She had a lovely smile on her face and was beaming. But why was she here, she explained she had taken her final sleep and all the pain had gone - it was exactly 11. 11. The next morning I was informed that my auntie had passed away at 11. 10 last night, her transition was sweet and her soul was now free for new adventures. Since this occurrence I know for sure that when people pass over they are immediately cured of all physical and mental illness there is no pain heaven can't heal.

Leaving school :

My first job was local and it seemed that I was to get my first wage packet. Real money to pay my way so to speak . It was during this period that my energies dropped so low. Each day a trial each night to be indured. Sleep was a very rare commodity. So many questions and very few answers. Sometimes I wished that I would go to sleep and not wake up. It would be very easy that way. No more voices and feelings of worthlessness - weeks passed turned into months the pain stayed ….on one cold winters night I laid awake pondering life or lack of it. A bright light entered my room followed by a clear vision of a Indian brave - this was my spirit guide, who I named “Feather” he became my life guide.

Many conversations would follow, we talked, we laughed, we cried - this partnership was made and created in heaven, for myself and the well being of all other lost souls. In me he saw pain and sufferring - real experience but also the promise of something far bigger and better “a new tomorrow”. Being different - he showed me what was good - breaking away from normality with the medicine of hope and comfort by my side this partnership was to set the foundation for a new path. One that would bring challenges and criticism but also a place outside the comfort zone together again - he showed me the mirror and the reason for living. First you must heal yourself - then help and guide desperate messages to be delivered to crying letterboxes .

Work helped so I could at least pay my way - but my heart was not really in it, weekends spent mostly - me alone with my special friends - an escape that would show me so much. A few changes of none descript jobs would follow. None felt right, just right at the time. I had bought myself some tarot cards and a few other items - spirit taught me - throw the book away – feel the cards - that way they will talk to you in such a manner - it seems natural and real. A few card readings would follow but invariably spirit took over delivered the messages that mattered. Meditations would bring in new friends but the art of music would bring in so much more the lyrics and rhythm can build bridges and give hope to the lost and weary.

I felt spirit by my side now and several readings would follow for friends of friends so to speak - One that sticks in my mind is for a 45 year old lady called Rose. She seemed distracted by my words and not really listening, I brought through her Mother - a hard stern lady, which brought little reaction from Rose. Then I felt the presence of a beautiful little girl come through - born with many problems and for the short time she was on the earth plain brought such fun and laughter – Rose ‘s hard exterior cracked and the tears of freedom washed through her heart. This little girl was free of all inhibitions and danced around her Mum lovingly.Rose thanked me like I had given her the world and just for a few moments the bridge of hope and comfort was open.

Chapter 2

Spirit levels :

My new job was shifts which enabled me to work with spirit on my time off. They would show me how to communicate on different levels - they truly knew they were the best of teachers for I was always in the moment and frequently simple but sure. Feeling down was still very much part of my personal life. I would wake up and my depression level was always very high. Just getting up and walking downstairs proved major obstacles. The only good part of my life was when spirit would ease my mind and take me to other levels. Regular visits to what I perceived to be heaven was common and this calmed my frantic mind. The best part of my physical life was when my consciousness was altered and the relentless pain in my mind would stop.

My work and life was good but very robotic I would often leave my body and I wander off to far away places. Close friends knew of my ability and would often seek advice on matters - however it was only for a few as I felt spirit talk within this environment would be frowned upon. Relationships would always prove difficult for me - I could often appear distant and this would mean three souls within the partnership. However I was to learn that loyalty within the relationship was critical and once broken could not be repaired. Being alone was natural to me - all my life I tried to fit in when really I just simply did not. When I realised that maybe I was destined to be on my own, life took on a new purpose - the one person you cannot lie to is yourself.

Spiritually I was growing which heralded me joining a circle. I joined an already competitive circle with all members confident with their abilities. Most weeks I would just listen to the other circle members giving accounts of their spiritual journey - very diverse and very different to my thinking. Most nights I would come home disenchanted and questioning of my ability - the group all knew each other and to be honest I tried but yet again I did not fit in. So I left the group I convinced myself what I was feeling it was all in my head and for now I was to walk away from spirit and get my head back into reality.

A few months would pass very slowly and yet again I became withdrawn from society. My solitude and loneliness the only companions. This was to change very quickly one day when a gentleman asked for my help his name was 'Mark'. Mark was a quiet man but very intelligent with a fantastic job in finance. I felt under pressure to deliver so as he sat in silence I turned to spirit. You could have cut the atmosphere with a knife but yet again spirit did not let me down. His brother came through who looked very similar to Mark - 'twins' he said loudly Mark stared anxiously. He talked of regret and of his tragic passing - he had taken his own life only three weeks ago. Tears ran down Mark's face he had been reunited with his twin brother. Further great evidence followed and the relief on Mark's face was profound. However souls pass to spirit they have the right to come back no matter what. Which was fitting really as I kept hearing 'No matter what' in my mind all through the reading coincidentally the song that was played as he left the church. I was back and spirit smiled.

'No ego'

Word WAS spreading and soon most weekends I was busy with my spirit work traveling out of the county on many occasions but always giving 100%. It seemed at last I had found something I was good at.

When I was not working with spirit I sat many years in the congregation of the local spiritualist church - watching other people receive messages gave me great joy. The nights I sat in the church waiting for that one message that would mean everything to me - but it was not to be and the proof I so desired never came.

My 1.2.1 Readings continued to grow and another local Medium asked me if I wanted to be part of a 'psychic super' in two weeks time. I accepted readily and joined seven other Mediums on that night. Each were drawn a table and that was ours for the night. As I was self taught (Spirit) I didn't know many other mediums so yet again I was the odd one out. I smiled and nodded to the other mediums most smiled back. But what I learned that evening stood me in good stead for all the years I have been a medium. So that is why in my mediumship I have no ego. How could I have everything what I have been given comes from spirit and likewise 'what is given' 'can also be taken away'. The night passed quickly but that lesson stays with me forever.

More of my workmates found out about my 'hidden talents' and asked about the lottery and that horse running at Doncaster this afternoon. I took it on the chin for this was work banter and saw it all as very comical.

Having tried the 'psychic supper' thing I decided my forte was 121 readings and these were beginning to take off again. I often travelled over the bridge and one dry but very cold winters evening I read for a lady called Amy. The reading had just began when I felt the energy of a man called Robert. A tall man with a small moustache he had passed with lung cancer at home. Amy nodded to my evidence but wanted more. He talked of his love for his wife and thanked her for caring for him. Amy burst into tears - she just wanted to know he was OK - Robert then began to sing - A fantastic voice and explained that he had sung at his own funeral. Amy explained they had played a track that Robert had recorded a couple of years back - so that night he definitely was 'King of the road'. It was late when I left and the stars shone brightly and it was approaching midnight as The Humber bridge came into sight the lady in the front of me had got out of her car I assumed she had broken down. I asked the attendant what the problem was it appears the lady had forgotten her purse. I walked over and saw a little baby in the car seat at the back. It was sub zero temperatures by now I walked over and paid the attendant for the lady and myself, she was so grateful and this is one of the few occasions in my life that touched my soul - on the way back my radio came on by itself the song ‘like a bridge over troubled waters’ played out spirit works in mysterious ways and it's better to believe than not, we can only do our best.

Chapter 3 :

Doubts and criticism

Doing what I do it's sometimes difficult as there is no script so to speak. Often doubt can come in and ruin a seemingly good message. Likewise we are always open to great criticism from the general public. So not understanding how the links works or how spirit come through can lead us to being called fraudulent.

However for all the people I have helped I have continued, often in the audience dragged along is the man who really did not want to be there. It is very strange that often as not this is the link you are drawn too. One such night occurred on my very first solo platform. Nerves were running through my body and taking control of my mind. But somehow I pulled myself together …with the ever present 'Feather' by my side I walked out to an expectant audience.

A quick sip of water and after a brief introduction from the host, the lights were on me 'breathe' said my loyal companion and I slowly began to utter my first words. I have always had a comical side to my Mediumship so I started with a joke. Amazingly people laughed and the release of the tension melted like frost on a sunny morning. Going right to the back I was drawn to a man with his arms folded and a look of complete boredom on his face. Why on earth would spirit take me to a man who obviously did not believe in this and would rather be at home eating is tea. I asked him if he could understand a man by the name of Dennis passed recently to the spirit world. He nodded nervously but the arms stayed folded in a 'stay away' mode. I needed to tread carefully I was with the right man but a non believer would only be tamed with the true facts. I felt it was his Dad but the spirit's apprehension did not help this sensitive link. I asked if he could take Dad in spirit 'yes' came the immediate answer. Dennis described the final words it had spoken to his much loved Son. He seemed that they had argued over something trivial and is Dad was offering an olive branch. The Son then spoke to confirm the facts and his arms relaxed and his face glowed - he had been reunited with his Dad? After the platform the man (Terry) came up to me - he said he thought this was a load of rubbish and people needed to get a life. But as he shook my hand strongly he said he was wrong. For now he could see his Dad again with a smile on his face all the negative energy had gone, and all the beautiful memories he had could shine again.

Sometimes doubt and fear can kill the greatest dreams. With Mediumship there is no set pattern or formula - I have learned sometimes that whatever you give will not be enough. Every reading is different and everyone open to scrutiny. There have been a few times when I have wondered what this is all about - the sheer criticism a nastiness can make you feel like walking away from spirit and never looking back. If we help people and heal how can it be so wrong. In these days of social media and the open Internet many can hide behind names of pain. But still through all of this I pushed on really not knowing where I was going.

But a belief that I could help people and make a real difference drove me on. They chose me for a reason and that alone meant so much to me. Someone had faith in me.

Mirror Mirror:

Having been a big believer in self taught my path was obvious - me and my thoughts against my spiritual journey - never did I think it would be such a tug of war with emotions and feelings major players. Some days I was just too low to try - I've never had great esteem and in the bad times just living was enough.

Alone with my thoughts sometimes I felt my head would explode - tired all day and awake all night was the usual pattern. I often thought it would be a great relief to me ... To just die. An ending to these constant fireworks in my head that never seemed to cease.

I remember one night sat on the edge of the bed for hours just staring at a mirror - wondering ... Who the hell was I? somehow on that night the mirror answered - behind me I could see glows of light which seemed strange - has no lights were on -Not really taking note of the significance I stared on drowning in my self pity. Then a face seemed to appear in front of mine. My senses became heightened and my heart began beating frantically. A younger man's features appeared in front of mine I was not scared more intrigued.

This was my first experience of personal trance - a pure connection to spirit with no middle man – the mirror showed me a young man about 25 called Steve. I suppose my empty mind and body what's a perfect vessel for a bit of evidential trance - realizing I was actually quite good at trance brought many hours of staring at a full length mirror. My voice although different would not speak in the native tongue of the excited spirit. This part of my personal journey showed me that giving up that little bit more would bring great rewards. It is true that this part of spiritual learning is so open to charlatans and fraud. But I carried on just me alone in my bedroom Full of spiritual apparitions. The art of Trance taught me so much. It was like talking to Elvis, rather than listening to his songs.

I began reading the auras of a few work colleagues and realised through the day how they could change dramatically. I still kept my abilities from the large workforce around me - my confidence was low and laughing and ridicule were not friends I wanted knocking at my door. My one to one readings were still coming in at a great pace and I felt humbled that so many had faith in me. Often after finishing several readings in one night I would feel so tired and low. Maybe I could have given more or tried for more evidence. It was one such night when I was driving home that spirit became my passenger. Surprised to see such a strong spirit beside me - I asked for clarity. It was a lady of 54 bright Brown eyes called Debbie. She had been part of the evening but I thought we had left our friends with the recipients. She asked 'why I was beating myself up so much 'surprised by her sharpness I chatted to her for the rest of the journey home. Suffice to say she filled me in on a few facts And what she told me stays with me until my dying day. Spirit need mediums to keep the bridge of hope and love - Forever open.

Spirit can be awkward and rude if that were the characteristics of the recipient. Spirit do not float on clouds or play harps, they would rather help and guide the needy. You cannot make people believe - To make a difference channel your energies into the ones where you can make a difference.

I pulled onto my drive and turned to say goodbye but she was gone. But her words stay forever - lighting the darkest nights.

Chapter 4

Grief:

Grief can take so long to overcome. It knows no boundaries nor does it leave anyone out. Many times I have been asked the question ? When does the pain stop? In truth there is no plain answer just that the time differs for us all. Sometimes we never get over it - we just get through it - one such case was when I read for a lady called Brenda - I arrived at her house one cool spring evening, as I pulled onto her drive I felt the presence of a quiet gentleman already with me. She welcomed me into her living room - I was met with countless photos of a man who had already made himself known. I started the reading and immediately a man called Dave came through. I explained I had felt his energy earlier and she smiled. He had passed some 10 years ago - but the room was a shrine. Dave quietly spoke of all the beautiful memories he had shared with Brenda. She began to dab tears away from her eyes as she shouted I've kept everything the same and your chair is still yours - no one sits in it !

Dave could see the pain was still there and it was her way of dealing with it. He explained that the love they shared and continue to share could never die. The photos, the chair, his own glass on the side were just material things. He asked Brenda to close her eyes, and then said 'can you still see me? she nodded and immediately realised what Dave was getting at. She did not need material things to hang on to Dave. Just her own mind full of beautiful memories.

The grief of the situation had kept her in the past and she did not want time to move on - Brenda thanked me so much for her reading - she knew now that the love of Dave would forever remain deep in her heart. She could move forward knowing that Dave could never come back for he had never left her.

In this reading I could see how we all deal differently with grief. I have often heard it said that mediums (who deal with the dead) do not feel the emotions and stresses of their practice. This is totally untrue and the reverse is much nearer the truth when a young man comes through who has taken his own life the extreme pain and suffering is immediately put onto the medium. Likewise the passing of any condition we feel it.

Sensitivity cannot be cut into two - you are either a sensitive or you're not. There has been many times when I've been in a large shop shopping centre where I've just needed to get out. The negative energies around were suffocating me. Likewise a death in the family is felt many times over. You can't become experienced and immune to death - you will have noticed in the last couple of pages have mentioned the word 'death'. This is a word that's thrown at all mediums "you talk two dead people don't you".

In reality we chat to there living souls - 'Tell us about heaven 'another often asked question - in reality 'heaven 'is in our own perception - very personal and individual.

Many are scared so ask these questions looking for something to hold onto so I probably feel I have been to heaven just the once - but with the countless criticism and backbiting in what I do, I have been to hell and back more times that I care to mention.

Chapter 5

Platforms :

More platforms would follow always very nervous and with great expectation. Music for me became my upliftment before the show. 'Ride a white Swan' by Marc Bolan always seem to resonate with me. I could not just sit and meditate this was not my way. A few minutes before the music would touch my soul and I was ready. No script - just a faith that they would not let me down. It was strange sometimes to see an audience all wanting me to come to them . There was no way I could satisfy each and everyone - all I could do was my best.

Sometimes so the briefest of moments I could see myself standing in front of a large audience and the fear and doubt would grab me. Thankfully this feeling would pass and it was on with the show.

I began on this particular night with a crazy joke or a view on life - this for me would break the ice and calm the nerves. I was so drawn to a man on the 3rd row - his wife was trying to make herself known - a small lady with a big character I felt - the name Kathy connected with this lady. The man looked up and nodded slowly I could see this was a recent passing. Kathy was asking how is back was - the man smiled he had twisted it this morning moving a cooker - spirit never cease to amaze me with the topical evidence to prove they are around us now. I heard the song 'Ben' by Michael Jackson and on asking this was her husband's name - the man I was drawn too - she talked of the long dark nights and countless cups of coffee.

Kathy had passed at home from stomach cancer and thanked Ben for his relentlessness care. She said all that was bad is gone and Ben smiled as a solitary tear ran down his cheek.

It was a lovely link to begin with and I felt warm inside - yet again the two lost souls had found themselves again. Most of my links last 6 – 8 minutes a time. My guide said this is long enough to give sufficient evidence. 'Feather' spoke of a boredom within the audience when links go on too long - and those words of wisdom stay with me every time I demonstrate.

Often during this time spirit would take over completely until the break - a bit like daydreaming through a maths lesson on a Monday morning. The times after a demonstration when people would come up and say that was my mum, dad, brother or sister - when in reality I had no great recollection of each separate message. It is impossible to remember each link there were too many.

I likened it to a dream you may have had last night and in the morning bits are there but by night all that remains is a feeling of waking up from a dream .

The next day after a platform I was always exhausted - the mental energy required to hold focus was off the scale. This left me open to the demons in my mind feeding me scraps from hell. I carried on knowing my only solitude were a few hours here and there of much needed sleep. Nights out with friends were OK but the world that I knew had far deeper and trusted souls. The many years I had been aware and worked with the spirit stood me in good stead. From this spiritual journey we are on can not be learned on a 'weekend with spirit 'or a two day tarot course. It's not a sprint it's a marathon after all certificates on walls means nothing without compassion and empathy.

I knew I still had much to learn but realised now that people would love me for what I am and not what they wanted me to be. A life lesson indeed.

Chapter 5

Doorkeeper :

Life was now pretty much on an even keel and spiritually I was growing every day. My main guide 'Feather' was by my side which meant so much to me. One to one readings were all watched over by his massive present. One particular night will forever remain in my memory I was reading for a man called Mark who lived 15 miles away. The reading was following it's normal path when out of nowhere I felt 'Feather' touch my shoulder. I found this strange as he had never done this before. He was stopping the reading. In my mind I asked him 'why'? I asked Mark for another glass of water to give me a few moments alone with 'Feather '.

It seemed that the recipient (Mark) was a non believer and was taken the reading to prove I was a fake and a hoax. A change of format was needed. Mark came back in the room and the reading re commenced. I felt the presence of a lady draw close called Carol - she shouted out the name of 'Will' - Mark did not take this. Again she said Will it's mum the look on Mark's face dropped. So I asked Mark "What was his real name?" 'Will' came back the answer a Reporter from the local paper - looking for a big story 'exposee unmasking the Mediums. He hadn't banked on his own mum coming through. He was flabbergasted and now totally apologetic. The whole energy changed it seemed his mum had died two years ago from bowel cancer.

Far more than a story ....he got his life back his mom came through with great evidence and Wills face just melted in emotion. My doorman had seen a problem and stopped the reading. It just goes to show you never know who or what you are reading for.

Just nice to know I have a spiritual filter watching over all things. I met Will some five years later at a petrol station - he came over and explained he was no longer a Reporter now he was working with underprivileged children at a centre. Quite a change he shook my hand and the world was good again.

The summer that year was long and hot and many nights when sleep seemed impossible we spent spiritually chatting – 'Feather' was a wise man with a boyish sense of humour - hence all my jokes during my presentation. I am honoured to have such a character for my spiritual guide. So Many times I have been asked to go bigger but this would not sit easily with what I wanted to do. I always wanted to appeal too people at grass roots and stay forever humble to who I really was. I never wanted fame in any window that just was not for me. I have always had a problem with the word 'Ego' - it always troubled me that I would let a God given ability change me into a demon.

I have already mentioned how for many years I sat in the congregation of the local spiritualist church - observing and watching the many mediums that would visit during the year. They taught me a lot and so my priorities now remain to be small but to appeal to large spectrum of people. To be forever approachable and always stay true to my humble beginnings - Mr ego can watch just like everyone else for I am just me scars and all and any inflated ego trips do not belong on my travel bus. And they will say 'he did his best with what he had' and for that legacy I rest very easy within my soul.

Chapter 6

Passing over :

The fact is with spirit and the spirit world if people choose not to believe that is their choice. Everyone is entitled to an opinion, some religions have different viewpoints and that's fine after all the world would become very boring if we all agreed on everything. I never advertised my services - at that time the people that came were either friends of friends or were drawn to me for a reason. One particular Saturday afternoon in May, I went for a 121 with a man called Edward - he welcomed me in but was very secretive and reserved. On entering his lounge area I felt a lady draw very close. On beginning the sitting I knew this was going to be a tricky reading. The lady spoke to me and said it was 'Emily ' she also spoke of her Roman Catholic upbringing. I felt that Edward too was Roman Catholic and indeed was a practicing priest. These facts slowly hit home with Edward and the relief was instant. Emily smiled and brought forward many facts of her life and passing. She was the wife of Edward for 30 years and relayed how happy they both were before being struck down with cancer. Edward accepted all the facts and realised that Emily was still very much part of his life. Edward explained that he just needed to know whether his beloved Emily was OK now.

His beliefs would normally have kept him away from people such as I - however he just needed to know - he thanked me on leaving and just like a switch had been turned on he was back in priest mode. He explained that we had never met and as such we were strangers.

In faith and humanity driving home I had time to take this reading in - very intricate but also very much needed.

Sometimes it is better not to question why just let the natural waves of life take place.

In life the bitter pills of trust and deceit are sometimes very hard to take - invariably being on your own although hard, is the easier option solitude and nature became my best friends on a path called loneliness.

I remember during my youth how I never really fitted in with society . It seemed these shadows yet again would try and steal my light. The spirit world would not let me go so easily. Leaving me for a few weeks to rest I was awoken one Sunday evening by a spirit at my bedside. A young boy smartly dressed and full of energy sat on the end of my bed. I asked who he was? The answer was chilling he said he was 'Oliver' but he wasn't dead yet. I thought how could this be possible - he explained he had a brain tumor and was in his last rites of life. He had slipped into a deep coma and was very close to passing over. I could not understand why spirit were showing me this But trusted there was a reason . I searched for answers but none came.

Some six weeks later I was travelling to a local football match and 'Oliver' appeared in my car again. He explained that he came through that night to show me that Mediums can pick up on the living when they are in an unconscious state. A lesson that taught me so much - within a whisker he had gone again.

The local match was proving entertaining and at half time I went for my warm up coffee - joining the queue I was soon at the front got my coffee and turned to return to my seat I was met with a man collecting money for a local charity - I gave him what change I had - the charity was for the brain tumor trust - the man had lost his son 'Oliver 'to this awful disease - answered from spirit.

All roads lead home :

We are all individual beings and likewise unique in the way we act and see life. So many copies instead of being the one beautiful you - often seeing success does not mean you need to follow that one exact path. Experiences of life teach us so much more than the screen or the book. Simply when it's felt we know.

Suicide is a subject but often comes through during a demonstration of mediumship. I have learned not too judge or comment just let the spiritual soul talk. So much pain left behind - it's hard to see a bridge, of hope love or anything. But come through they do and I honour there souls like any other. I give out my evidence and look who I am drawn to. The spirit is not weak it's strong as is the message shining through. A name, a date, something of consequense the recipient holds on to every crumb

Analysing and trying to understand. I feel the anguish and stress in the moment I see options a few and I see the door marked 'exit'. Now it's time to rebuild for a new tomorrow and just starting an healing process means so much.

The room left untouched the clothes still in the wardrobe - how can spirit begin to explain - one such soul came through on a Friday evening in November - he came early on at the beginning of the night - bringing heavy metal music has his backing track 'Chris 'made himself known. He shouted that his Mum and Sister where in the audience - I was drawn to near the back. Two very reserved recipients nodded in anticipation. Chris loved his music and had played guitar in a local band. Mum and sister were now perched on the end of the seat - Chris firstly offered a profound 'sorry 'for all the pain he had caused. He went onto explain the pain in his mind was just too much. Details of the tragic night followed all verified by two weeping family loved ones. Then he spoke to his sister directly the 'don't give up' message was strongly passed on. She seemed to understand it - then he said 'mum you don't have to visit my grave every day , I'm in every sunset and every star.' His mum smiled with tears running down her face she had reconnected with her son. Tomorrow was a new day.

His sister came up at the end to add light to the 'don't give up 'message it seems they had been trying for a family for five years now - but to no avail. They both thanked me and we all went our separate ways - the night were successful but my energies as always were very low.

I slept through to the morning - for once my mind gave me a little peace. Some six months after the demonstration I was in the local shopping centre I walked straight into the two ladies again - they both smiled and we exchanged pleasantries - just before leaving his sister said she had just been in 'mother care' to buy some clothes for her forthcoming baby. My heart smiled and I felt Chris's message again 'don't give up '. In extreme pain they had found love and the family was whole again.

I drove home with a smile on my face , so nice when things work out. Putting on the car radio I listened letting it calm my tired mind - and lo and behold 'highway to hell 'came on. The same song Chris had played to make himself known. One more rainbow to drive away the rain.

Chapter 7

Spirit talk :

Sensitivity for Mediums is a double edged sword. It is much needed in a platform or 121 readings - however on the negative side it can evoke all kinds of demons - some saying you're not worthy or fraudulent. This side stays with you forever part of you but not all you . In this modern society we are always open for put down or criticism. Sometimes when you demonstrate mediumship you just know that the recipient will say 'no ' no matter what do you give them - one such event happened at a private house party. My friend had invited me to come along and do a night of spirit links at his house 12 miles away. It was a Saturday and I arrived about 7:00 p.m. The party was in full flow with food and drink a plenty. He had a large living room and when I entered 20 people were waiting expectantly. Seating was crammed and one man (Colin) was sat on the carpet about 6 feet away. He was not drunk but suffice to say he was merry.

My first few links were Ok and taken - Colin seem to take great fun in saying 'general rubbish 'after each comment. The night followed the same line good links (Colin's)imput was proving hard. We had a little break midway and I had a well earned cup of tea. We were now in the kitchen and I could see 'Colin' making a beeline for me with another countless tinny in his hand. I was polite and smiled as he told me he did not believe in this sort of thing. He had only come along for the food and drink. Anyway leaving me alone for awhile he had left me with 'when you're dead you're dead' I gave myself 10 minutes - My guide smiled at me and we returned to the room.

The night continued along the same vein and then I announced that the next link was to be my last. Colin was off again 'thank God for that 'then we can see some real spirit he shouted. 'Feather drew close and I knew this was going to be a special link. I would like to come to the lovely quiet gentleman sat but six feet away from me. Everyone laughed except Colin. My link was a tall man with a moustache he shouted out 'Col are you listening '. For the first time in the whole evening the room fell silent. My link made himself known has 'Steve ' best friend of Colin. Steve had passed in a traffic accident two years ago. Colin accepted all the facts with a disbelief and he seemed to sober up in a moment. Tears ran down Colin's cheeks - in a show of emotion that touched the whole room. Steve laughed and his leaving message was 'am not dead I live on in all the beautiful memories we shared together. Obviously re addressing Colin's line off 'when you're dead , you're dead.

I thanked everyone for coming and said my goodbyes to all who attended. I had left my coat in the kitchen so went to collect it - before leaving Colin approached me with tears in his eyes and shook my hand so strongly. He could not let me leave without thanking me personally - he was like a changed man, could this really be the man who had ridiculed me but one hour before.

On the drive home 'Feather' spoke to my mind - he talked of ignorance and sheer bitterness in this world. The night was a massive learning curve but the experience stays with me forever. I am just one man trying to spread a little light in the times of darkness - CAN that really be so wrong?

Lifes jewels :

Spiritually we are all very complex and to a large extent on very different paths. I have always believed that we all take with us are two things - firstly the experience of living an human life on this planet and secondly the love we have shared with our special family and friends - no material things get through life's filters so that posh house and car get left behind - Thrown out just like the Christmas tree at the beginning of January.

I also believe when you first meet someone you pretty much workout if you will get on with them in the initial first 30 seconds. It's to do with auras and souls blending. I have shared platforms with so many fantastic mediums, and learned so much from them and for that I will always be eternally grateful.

But for me and the way I deliver mediumship I feel I am so much better on my own - it's just me the audience and the inspiring spirit world.

One to one readings I feel is where you are really earn your skills - just the one recipient means you need to go deeper to find life jewels. One such reading was when I read for a man called Geoff. a proud 74 year old pensioner with a glint in his eye. I read for him at his home one autumn afternoon. I brought through his mum and dad and he chuckled about all the memories. Then I brought through his lovely wife Margaret who had passed sadly some 20 years ago. His face lit up on recalling all the loving memories. Several other family members and friends also came to the party. It was so lovely to feel their beautiful energies that Geoff was happy so many spirit friends had come through - but I sensed a sadness in his eyes - was there something I had missed? as I got up to leave I felt a small dog at my feet - a beautiful Jack Russell from the spirit world jumped on to Geoff's lap - I passed this information on and Geoff began to cry uncontrollably. This was the message he so desired – Geoff explained his loyal best friend 'skip 'lived with him for 15 years. A few days ago he had become unwell and gone off his legs - the trip to the vets was not a good one 'skip ' was shutting down - sadly he had to be put to sleep the trip to the vets was only yesterday, but his loyal beautiful companion was not passing up the chance to come back – and here he was in all his glory. Geoff now had some closure. The Rainbow Bridge had opened and the world was good again.

So many links came through on that day but the one that really mattered so much came through at the end. This spiritual journey we are all on never ceases to amaze me.

The years would slowly tick by and it was only at the end of each ones readings that I realised how many I had actually done - On a couple of occasions I was approached by the police connections to offer my thoughts on certain matters. Each time I declined my guide 'feather' informed me this was a slippery slope full of ridiculed and heartache along the way. Enquiries would follow also about 'haunted houses and ghost walks'. Neither was a path that I intended to walk. They were just not right for me but realise some Mediums go down this route and perform great work.

I decided to set up my own Facebook page 'Tom J. King 'to help people or just to give them an insight into the spirit world. A few select people would join as it was a private group - often a few jokes and a passing insight would fill my pages. It was not intended to make me bigger - just better. A new shop window to help and guide - but for me the start of a new tomorrow.

Chapter 8

'Rita'

Time was rolling by quickly now and the bookings were coming in steadily. Different venues as well - one such one was a local venue I had not been to before. It was for a psychic supper - me three other Mediums. Someone called 'Rita Moody' had rung up and she was my contact. It was a small room but it felt very cozy with candles on every table. Each Medium would have a set time at each table and then move around. So by the end of the night each Medium would have visited each table. It was a good night time passed really quickly .

Afterwards we all enjoyed some much needed food Rita was a wonderful host and looked after us all attentively.

Spirit shone so many quick sharp messages were given - Good feedback meant there would be more visits back to this lovely venue.

In 2014 another new venue 'Transformation Rita Moody' was the owner and I was to take a 'night of mediumship' When I arrived Rita was already there so we chatted openly over a cup of tea. The place seemed very spiritual and quaint.

The links came easily that night and before long the evening was over - I stayed behind to help tidy up and it was 11:30 before I left - I said my goodbyes and I was on my way home. Myself and Rita had a bond - of course very spiritual but more than that could I after all the heartache have found someone for me - Time would tell.

The next year myself and another medium did a large charity event. It was very well attended - a sellout in fact -

we had chairs everywhere. I remember standing on the stage and looking out thinking gosh so many people - the night was so successful and together we raised lots of money for charity. Rita's admin skills and attention to detail meant the night passed without a hitch.

Myself and Rita got closer and closer and soon I was proud to call her my beautiful partner. To be honest I thought I was destined to go through life alone. She showed me so much love but I was sure spirit had had a hand in bringing us together. Now with a personal secretary (Rita) the 121s were flying in and spirit seemed to be smiling at me again .

One such reading was for a lady called 'Francis' an elderly woman but she had real presence about her - her husband 'Albert' came through really quickly he had a stick and spoke very quickly. Francis nodded to the evidence - soon he was talking about an operation to an hip that was needed. Francis said she had a date for the operation in four weeks - Albert drew so close to his wife I could feel that Francis knew he was there - some love you see can never die - it just lives on forever. Francis was so pleased with the reading she thanked me and left the room - my reading room now was at 'Transformation' and the clients were now coming to me.

All those years chasing all over the country taking me to breaking point both mentally and financially - Rita even got me a sign for my reading room - God bless her.

Platforms at transformation sold out immediately we just needed another venue - Rita looked to book the local village hall - so much bigger And so much more space - with Rita by my side this was a new dawn .

The spirit world smiled and waited with baited breath for the next installment.

Chapter 9

Choices :

There is no doubt in this world we have choices between good and bad - in fact you could say that our lives are full of choices. Sometimes spirit will lead you to the door but it's up to us to walk through it. I never really saw myself walking on stage alone in front of a large audience - but there I was hall full waiting for me and spirit to deliver .

It was a Friday night in September and to say I was feeling nervous was putting it mildly. Cometh the hour Cometh the man. Being in the spotlight brought fear and excitement in equal measures - my legs literally had turned to jelly - hopefully I could string a few words together and begin.

Thankfully a beautiful lady joined me on stage immediately. Pressure released she said it was 'Greta' and she was mum to someone in the audience. I was drawn to a lady midway and at the end of a row. The recipient came back with a strong 'I can take that' Greta gave me so much evidence it was hard to defy it. She also brought with her a beautiful Labrador dog - the animal kingdom is always welcome in my presentations. It was a lovely message and yet again I felt humbled that I could pass on such messages of hope and love.

My first half was always just me and spirit delivering as many messages as possible. My guide 'feather' always said 7 to 8 minutes is long enough to give sufficient evidence. Telling me a big audience would become 'bored' if I stayed too long on a link. I always listened to my guide he was and is my ultimate teacher.

The second half was slightly different I would use music to bring through the links on a bridge of upliftment and rhythm. Prior to any demonstration I would be given tunes of purpose and rememberence. These could vary from World War Two war songs to modern day hip hop. Just listening to them could bring so much raw emotion. I did not know why I used certain songs just a trust that radio spirit FM would not let me down.

Many times just playing a song to a quiet audience does evoke such passion and emotion within. However I can only go to the person I am drawn to with my spirit sat nav. This night it was a man on the 2nd row - often when I go to a recipient the shy quiet switch is turned on. I felt I had a man with me who would have worn glasses and near the end have a stick. It was a 'Dad' and connected with the name 'Bruce' - the man on the 2nd row took all the information and now was openly conversing with me - No matter what evidence is given the recipient always craves more. But once I get my tap on the shoulder from my guide I know I am nearing the end of my link.

At the end of my demonstration people would often walk up to me and thank me for their link. Often questions would follow about my link with Mum/Dad/Sister Etc. But in reality when each personal message has been given I have no great recollection or memory left in my mind. It just doesn't work like that for me. Just for a few moments I have a glimpse into other lives but this does not stay with me. I liken it to a dream that you cannot remember first thing in the morning. But as the day goes on the thoughts become less and less and by night most have melted like a snowman in the sun.

I have learned giving messages its the little things that count and every memory has a place in someone's heart.

Workshops :

The spirit world never let you rest on your laurels and soon they pushed me into teaching. A sharing of my experiences and bringing forward the future Psychics and Mediums is the way the spirit world see it.

So soon I was planning workshops on colour and working with music. The truth is we all have our own paths to follow - each unique and individual - workshops gives the opportunity to learn new skills and develop the abilities we already have. Also the chance to chat to like minded people without the fear of put down and ridicule.

I believe when we go through life we are often thrown things that we don't understand . As spiritual beings trapped in a physical body it's obvious this can puzzle greatly at times .

My spiritual teachings have always been flavoured with a bit of humour. This subtle and gentle way often leads to such great results. Not everyone that comes to my workshops have a passion to be a Medium or a Psychic and that is absolutely fine.

Life has taught me that understanding who we are is one of the great tasks we face. I have seen people who have 'everything 'with great sadness behind their eyes. Likewise people who have very little can resonate such happiness.

Workshops also can build a bond within them where trust and confidence can flow very easily. I am a big believer in colour and the use of it at appropriate times. When we are feeling down we talk of 'blue' – 'red' is often used for aggression - and we all know that the colour black is associated with 'funerals'.

I believe that simple colour scan change our moods. Sensory rooms for children with autism are always bright colours to lift up and connect. What we wear can also determine what we are feeling. The most spiritual colour purple was used by UKIP in all of the adverts during the past election.

So standing in front of students and giving out spiritual teachings was very much part of my personal development. Not everything you say will resonate with them - however if I gave you a couple of 'light bulb ' moments then my job was done.

Sitting with like minded people also allows you the opportunity to hear other peoples opinions and do that one thing called 'listen'. There may come a time where you may want to 'sit in a circle'. This will help your development. Just make sure you find one that suits your energies. I have taken a few and continue to sit in them. We never stop learning or evolving - I was now using more of my abilities and I felt the spirit was with me every stage.

I always felt to that within the workshops I learned so much from the students. It was so interesting seeing their viewpoint on different exercises. I always felt that meditation is an important part of development - however it was not the be all and end all of everything. I loved exercises to get the mind working and got great results from them. My style of teaching is not for everyone and it's certainly not textbook by any means. However I did feel that the students benefitted from my energetic approach - now I decided again to look at trance and all it's undeniable ways - giving up that little more to connect to spirit in a pure way made my soul warm.

Chapter 10

Trance:

It was a cold winters night when I decided to show Rita my skills of Trance. For years I had sat in front of a large mirror allowing spirit to come through. I explained to her that even though my persona and facial features may change I was fine and it was only part of the Trance. I sat relaxed on the sofa and explained to Rita what was about to happen. It was my intention to allow the spirit world in using me as a vessel. My breathing would alter and in time hopefully ectoplasm from the mouth and nose would form a face in front of mine.

I would allow the spirit to over shadow and go into a trance like state - this in no way is possession but I had taken years to perfect the ability to trance. Some light music was put on in the background to calm and relax and I was ready. The room was lit with candles which meant Rita could clearly see my face - she sat about six foot away from me and I asked her to interact with the spirit when and if anything came through.

What follows is Rita's words on the night 'Tom 'sat quietly for a few minutes the only change being his breathing which became slower and laboured. I noticed is head looking around the room like surveying a parking place - the temperature in the room seemed to change but I was not scared or anxious - Tom then started to mutter I could not work out the words at first - then his voice became deeper and more profound - his face seemed to be surrounded by a thin mist and the mist was forming the features of my beautiful Mum. What transpired next was both amazing and surreal. Myself and my Mum had a full blown conversation about anything and everything. I could smell her perfume filling the room these moments for me were surely from another world - we talked of family past and present and memories we shared that no one would know about. Tom seemed relaxed and calm throughout. My Mum was truly in the room when it was time to say goodbye I did not want it to end. However those treasured moments stay with me forever.

Tom slowly came back into the room oblivious of the magic he had brought through. This was a remarkable night for me I listened to Rita's account and was completely amazed. Prior to the trance beginning I told Rita it would last about 40 minutes. The link finished spot on like finishing a phone call - the power of spirit that night totally blew me away. Since then I have 'tranced' through several relatives of recipients. Sometimes with spirit it's better to just go with it then trying to look for answers all the time. Many times I have been asked 'prove that is spirit ' my answer is always the same 'you prove am not' and of course they can't.

Slowly psychic and mediumship is now being accepted in society. I do believe that even with a life times experience I am only just touching the surface - So you can keep your online diplomas and weekend retreat certificates I'm sure they look lovely on the wall. It's not a science you learn in class or on a P.C it's all about living experiences the ups and downs - when you learn this you are on the 1st stepping stone. Compassion and empathy run in tandem with your newly found awareness.

Chapter 11

'Crystal clear'

But what of the famous spirits that passed away - Elvis - lady Di - Michael Jackson - do they ever come through? And my answer is yes to the people who knew them. I have heard it said many times that Michael Jackson came through during a seance or Elvis tipped the table over. Sorry but that belongs with the Easter Bunny and Jack Frost. The job of a Medium means you must also be a good therapist for sometimes it is not the message - but the way you say the message. You should not leave a client upset or in a state of disarray. Sometimes the client wants to talk - let them talk - you may be the only one listening. I am aware that sometimes the recipient of a message can become very vulnerable - so tread gently we are supposed to be mending them not breaking. Tears are a great release of things we have hung on to - often leading to a feeling of being 'able to move on'.

Often when we lose a little faith we look to maybe a bit of backing from the spirit world. Such a message came through when I read for a lady called 'Monica' she wasn't to sure about this sort of thing but wanted to give it a try. Monica's Dad 'Bill' came through straight away - he had been in the spirit world some 10 years and passed with a heart attack with no warning whatsoever. Monica accepted the evidence but looked quite brittle, 'Bill' Firstly wanted to say but she would always be his 'girl' and missed her so much. He went on to say that he 'felt' enough was enough and it was time to leave - Monica explained her relationship had gone wrong and she did not know what to do. Her Dad spoke honestly and the words 'leopards don't change the spots ' run true with her she now knew what to do the advice from her beloved Dad was crystal clear. In a way she looked relieved that a decision had now been made - she thanked me and the reading was over. We are always looking for reassurance and in this reading it came from a very reliable source.

I am often asked 'why if your so good have you not ever won the lottery' well in reality it's not about self gain it's about guiding - helping and just being there - people often say 'I have some Tarot cards' – 'can I read for myself?' And the answer is yes - however if you have a bad day and your energies are low that is what will come through the cards. So set your ambience light some candles - silence your mind and go for it.

I know several people who like to use the pendulum for life's questions and that's fine - just realise that some questions cannot simply be answered with a yes or no. Personally I would be careful with the pendulum as our own minds make up the answer long before the question. The spirit world I believe runs parallel with this world rather like the weather.

-Videos pictures and photos all bring back memories - however our minds hold the greatest Golden threads. I often ask a recipient to close their eyes – 'now can you see the passed over loved ones? - On most occasions they come back with 'yes' then they are still with you. There is no secret formula for connecting to spirit. Just what works for you. They can heal most wounds and our minds can turn a negative into a positive we must not over annalyse what spirit gives us. Love and hope do not need fancy boxes.

Real again :

So what do spirit lack when they come through? Well they are everything they were before just without the human body they owned whilst on the physical plain. So if they were out spoken and loud - that's how they would come through - I do not believe the soul and the characteristics of the person changes else how would we recognise them.

During my demonstration you will often hear me use the term 'make spirit real' this means just because their physical life is over the rest is the same. So when we use the term 'lost' then this is not the case. We are all eternal and live on. Sometimes the grief is so powerful that it supersedes all other feelings and emotions. So when a medium reconnects with your loved one this makes the whole person real again. The negative thoughts of the person can be dramatically erased this showed up when I did a reading for a man called 'Derek ' he sat across from me with a gaze that said nothing - I could feel the emptiness in his heart - a man broken - I could feel the energy of a lady draw close to him - this was his wife 'Grace' who had passed over five years ago - she asked 'why have you kept all my clothes? Derek look up and told me it was because he was beginning to forget what she looked like looked like - and more worrying for him could not hear her voice anymore. Grace spoke back 'our memories of love will keep me alive' I explained to Derek that hanging on to material things were keeping the negative thoughts of the passing alive - go outside and see 'Grace 'in every new morning. Derek realised he had created a morbid shrine to 'Grace 'and this was stopping the light of her real memory coming through. Derek smiled again and the world lifted from his tired shoulders. The thing is we create our own reality in our own minds - and what we believe is real - is real.

There have been so many questions asked during my life as a Medium one of the most common is - my loved one did not believe in this stuff will they still come through? And the answer on every occasion undeniably 'yes' a gateway or door is still there whether you can see it or not .

Healing from spirit is a beautiful thing whether you believe its going to rain - you still get wet - love does not judge - nor does it have a face. Leaving a legacy of sun and laughter is a beautiful thing. People will always remember how you made them feel. Try always to be kind for each of us have our demons. And they can reoccur at anytime in any place.

The fantastic animal Kingdom often comes through during my 121 readings and demonstrations. We could all learn so much from them - firstly they love unconditionally - no limits - also they are so loyal - such loyalty we often seek in humans. They are all so psychic more than we will ever know - dogs and cats have been used to detect cancer in humans - often tapping the area of concern. Over the years I have brought through too many to mention I feel like doctor dolittle at times. I feel extremely honoured that they willingly participate in my readings. The extreme power of our pets should never be underestimated and they are always welcome during my readings .

We all see the world differently and choose our friends along the way - we never lose them - memories remain good or bad they make us what we are today. The spirit world embrace everything and we all know that somewhere between tomorrow and forever we will meet again.

Chapter 12

Table service :

Thinking now as I approach my Golden years where will spirit take me next. In all honesty it was spirit who pushed me into writing this book. I am not a natural author but they wanted it writing down. A legacy there forever for someone or anyone to read. It's all my opinions and thoughts from working with spirit for so long - often during the writing of the book I would just put the pen on the line and wait for inspiration. We all seek perfection and set ourselves targets that are just not reachable. Far better to live in the moment and see what is now .

One very special reading lives on in my memory - it was in my very early years of readings but taught me so much - one cold Saturday afternoon in October I travelled to a ladies home some 25 miles away her name was 'Lucy ' and she welcomed me into her house - the reading began as normal with me asking Lucy to relax and enjoy the reading. A man drew close by the name of 'Larry' he said it was 'Dad ' that had passed in an accident 20 years ago. Lucy accepted the information with a smile - she asked me if he was 'ready' which puzzled me - nothing came back from 'Larry' - all he showed me was a table with people around it - Lucy thought for awhile then she shouted 'I get it' well I was pleased she did I was getting more and more confused. Then A tall man with a beard stood by her side connected with the name 'Terry' Lucy smiled again and explained that was her husband who passed two years ago. Terry spoke Anne said 'the usual place' Lucy nodded well I felt like the reading was in a foreign language totally – confused.com. Lucy seemed now more at ease which was nice to see. She asked of her future so I took out my loyal tarot cards laid them out and nothing. What was going on? The spirit world had shut down and I began to feel increasingly sick. Lucy did not seem concerned - rather than disappointed she appeared happy .

I left feeling really down not knowing what the hell was going on, two weeks later she texts me out of the blue - she had my number from the booking. She explained the reading to me, Lucy had terminal cancer - but had been in remission - she knew very well that she did not have long - when her dad came through and asked if she was ready - it was regarding to her passing. The table was to show her place with family members already there. And with her husband Terry the 'usual place ' showed they were all ready and waiting. This gave her great comfort to know that her dad and husband were already at the bus stop so to speak. The tarot reading or lack of it showed Lucy her passing was close - everything dropped into place - some 10 days later I received a text from Lucy's phone it was her sister, she had passed over during the night. I smiled and reminded myself of her face when I brought through her dad and husband. The table was again complete and spirit taught me the greatest of lessons - that afternoon I put on my radio the song playing was 'come to the table ' Sidewalk Prophets ' - how lovely to know she had been reunited.

The spirits will always be around and I will always be in awe of their Supreme power.

This book was wrote with their help and guidance - I hope to some it will show them the light and to others the thought that maybe there is more. Live your life the best you can and to use your God given talents to make this world a better place.

Afterword:

So my book is finished - good or bad I hope it makes a difference in your life. Thank you to all that have helped me along my rollercoaster path. I especially wanted to thank my partner Rita Moody who gave me belief when all was gone - and faith when the shadows of criticism and doubt raised their ugly heads.

The spirit world chose me for this task and for that I will be eternally grateful and now approaching my Golden years I will continue on my path wherever it may lead me. Time does not stand for anyone and nor should it.

I hope that the writing of this book does justice to the power of the spirit and I must thank them all for being my constant companions .

In life we must follow our own standards and always try to be nice and kind. This troubled world we live in so needs it - God bless and remember - you never lose, you either win or learn.

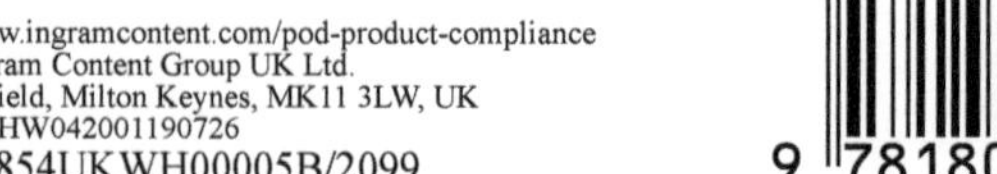

www.ingramcontent.com/pod-product-compliance
Ingram Content Group UK Ltd.
Pitfield, Milton Keynes, MK11 3LW, UK
UKHW042001190726
13854UKWH00005B/2099

9 781800 312968